COI

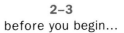
MW01155850

British & North American Readers:
Please note that Australian cup and
spoon measurements are metric. A quick
conversion guide appears on page 63.
A glossary explaining unfamiliar terms
and ingredients begins on page 60.

2 before you begin...

*Follow these important gems of information and
successful preserves are guaranteed!*

helpful hints
• Fruit and vegetables used for
preserving must be unblemished
and well washed.
• Always use good-quality vinegars
containing at least 4% acetic
acid; cheaper vinegars do not
contain enough acetic acid to
act as a preservative.
• We have used minimal salt in our
recipes. Taste the preserve before
bottling; add salt to suit your taste.

Sterilising jars and treated lids on the stovetop

• When making preserves, use
large, wide-topped saucepans or
boilers made of either aluminium
(providing the preserve is not left
standing in the pan for more than
an hour), stainless steel or enamel.
Never use copper or unsealed
cast-iron pans; the acid in the
preserve will damage the metal,
and colour and flavour ingredients.

jars and bottles
• Jars and bottles must be made
of glass, without chips or cracks,
and should be thoroughly washed,
then sterilised. Keep jars covered
with a clean tea-towel to keep dust-
free while preparing preserves.
Jars and bottles must be dry. Make
sure your hands and tea-towels
are clean. Unclean jars can cause
deterioration in preserves.

Sterilising methods
Method 1: Put clean jars and lids
in dishwasher, put through rinse
cycle at hottest temperature;
do not use detergent.
Method 2: Place clean jars on their
sides in large saucepan or boiler,
cover completely with cold water;
place lid on pan, bring to a boil.
Boil, covered, 20 minutes. Carefully
remove jars from water – tongs
are useful for this. Drain jars well

then stand, right-way up, on clean wooden board. The heat from the jars will cause any remaining water to evaporate.

Method 3: Wash jars well in hot soapy water; rinse thoroughly in hot water to remove all traces of soap. Stand clean jars, right-way up and not touching, on clean board in cold oven; turn oven temperature to very slow, leave for 30 minutes. Remove jars from oven.

sealed and delivered

• As soon as hot preserves are spooned into sterilised jars or bottles, they must be correctly sealed to prevent deterioration.
• Fill jars right to the top, as preserves shrink slightly on cooling. If sealing with paraffin wax, leave space for the wax to be poured over the preserve.
• Metal lids are not suitable; the acid content of the preserve will corrode the lids and the contents become contaminated. Special lined and treated or lacquered lids,

available with home preserving outfits, are suitable to use.
• Plastic screw-top lids give a good seal (plastic snap-on lids are not airtight enough). Plastic lids must be well washed, rinsed and dried, or put through the dishwasher.
• Some older preserving outfits have glass lids; these can be sterilised by any of the above methods. Do not use aluminium foil, cellophane or paper covers for preserves; acid in the preserves will corrode foil, while paper and cellophane are not airtight enough for long-term keeping.
• Paraffin wax makes an excellent seal. Melt slowly in small saucepan over low heat; pour a thin layer, about 2mm thick, just enough to cover surface of preserve. Leave until almost set, then pour another thin layer on top of first layer. Insert small pieces of string in wax just before it sets to make it easier to remove wax. It is important not to overheat wax or it will shrink on cooling, giving an imperfect seal.

Sterilising jars and lids in the dishwasher

Drying jars and lids on wooden board

apple, choko and date chutney

This chutney is an excellent accompaniment to cheese or cold meats, and is also delicious served with a curry.

2 large chokoes (700g), peeled, chopped

3 tablespoons salt

8 medium apples (1.2kg), peeled, chopped

2 large brown onions (400g), chopped

1 litre (4 cups) brown vinegar

2 fresh red Thai chillies, seeded

1/2 cup (80g) sultanas

1/2 cup (85g) dates, chopped

4 cloves garlic, crushed

2 tablespoons ground ginger

2 teaspoons five-spice powder

1 tablespoon ground turmeric

1 tablespoon mixed spice

2 dried bay leaves

1kg (5 cups) firmly packed brown sugar

Place chokoes in large bowl, sprinkle with salt; leave overnight. Rinse chokoes well under cold water; drain. **Combine** apple, onion, vinegar, chillies, sultanas, dates and choko in large saucepan; simmer, covered, about 10 minutes or until soft. Add remaining ingredients; simmer, uncovered, about 1½ hours or until thick and rich-brown in colour. Remove bay leaves and chillies; pour into jars, seal while hot.

MAKES 2.5 litres (10 cups)
Per tablespoon 0g fat; 167kJ
Storage In cool, dark place about 6 months; refrigerate after opening

6 date and tamarind relish

75g dried tamarind

2 cups (500ml) boiling water

2 teaspoons vegetable oil

2 teaspoons black mustard seeds

2 teaspoons cumin seeds

500g fresh dates, seeded, chopped coarsely

1/4 cup (60ml) malt vinegar

Combine tamarind and the water in medium heatproof bowl. Cover; stand 30 minutes.
Strain tamarind over small bowl, pressing to extract all liquid; discard tamarind.
Heat oil in medium heavy-base saucepan; cook seeds, stirring, until they pop. Stir in dates, tamarind liquid and vinegar; bring to a boil. Simmer, uncovered, stirring occasionally, about 5 minutes or until mixture is almost dry. Blend or process mixture until almost smooth.
Spoon hot relish into hot sterilised jars; seal while hot.

MAKES about 2 1/2 cups (625ml)
Per tablespoon 0.4g fat; 103kJ
Storage In refrigerator for about 2 weeks

quince paste

You need to use a long-handled wooden spoon and wrap your arm in a clean tea-towel for the final stages of the cooking of quince paste, as it will burn badly if it comes in contact with your skin.

2kg quinces, peeled

1.75kg (8 cups) caster sugar

½ cup (125ml) lemon juice

Quarter quinces and core; reserve cores. Wrap cores in piece of muslin; place in large boiler with quince and enough cold water to cover quince. Bring to a boil, reduce heat; simmer, covered, until quince is soft and most liquid is absorbed (quince should now be ruby-red in colour, depending on variety and ripeness of quince used). Discard cores; mash quince in boiler.
Measure quince pulp; add 1 cup (220g) caster sugar for each cup of pulp. Stir in juice; stir over low heat, without boiling, until sugar is dissolved. Bring to a boil; boil, stirring constantly, about 40 minutes or until mixture is very thick. Spoon mixture into hot sterilised jars; seal while hot.

MAKES about 8 cups (2 litres)
Per tablespoon 0g fat; 322kJ
Storage In cool dark place for up to 1 year; refrigerate after opening

8 basic tomato ketchup

1 teaspoon black peppercorns

6 whole cloves

1 bay leaf

8 large tomatoes (2kg), chopped coarsely

2 medium white onions (300g), chopped coarsely

½ cup (125ml) red wine vinegar

1 cup (220g) sugar

2 teaspoons coarse cooking salt

1 tablespoon tomato paste

Tie peppercorns, cloves and bay leaf in piece of muslin. Place muslin bag in large heavy-base saucepan with tomato and onion; bring to a boil. Simmer, uncovered, stirring occasionally, about 45 minutes or until onion is soft. Discard bag. Cool mixture 10 minutes.

Blend or process mixture until smooth; strain through fine sieve back into same pan. Add remaining ingredients; stir over heat, without boiling, until sugar dissolves. Simmer, uncovered, stirring occasionally, about 15 minutes or until mixture thickens to desired pouring consistency.

Pour hot ketchup into hot sterilised bottles or jars; seal while hot.

MAKES about 1.25 litres (5 cups)

Per tablespoon 0.1g fat; 87kJ

Storage In cool, dark place for about 6 months; refrigerate after opening

4 large red onions
(1.2kg), sliced

1½ cups (375ml)
water

½ cup (125ml)
malt vinegar

⅔ cup (130g) firmly
packed brown sugar

2 teaspoons finely
grated orange rind

½ cup (125ml)
orange juice

Combine onion and the water in large
saucepan, bring to a boil; boil, uncovered,
stirring occasionally, about 20 minutes or until
onion is soft and liquid has evaporated.
Add remaining ingredients; stir over heat,
without boiling, until sugar is dissolved.
Simmer, covered, 30 minutes. Remove cover,
simmer, stirring occasionally, further 30 minutes
or until mixture thickens. Spoon marmalade into
hot sterilised jars; seal while hot.

MAKES about 2 cups (500ml)
Per tablespoon 0.1g fat; 162kJ
Storage In refrigerator for about 1 month

10 tomato chutney

8 medium tomatoes (1.5kg)

3 medium white onions (450g), chopped finely

1½ cups (300g) firmly packed brown sugar

1½ cups (375ml) malt vinegar

1½ tablespoons mustard powder

1 tablespoon mild curry powder

½ teaspoon cayenne pepper

2 teaspoons coarse cooking salt

Peel and coarsely chop tomatoes; combine with remaining ingredients in large heavy-base saucepan. Stir over heat, without boiling, until sugar dissolves. Simmer, uncovered, stirring occasionally, about 1¼ hours or until mixture thickens.

Spoon hot chutney into hot sterilised jars; seal while hot.

MAKES about 1 litre (4 cups)
Per tablespoon 0.1g fat; 139kJ
Storage In cool, dark place for about 6 months; refrigerate after opening

beetroot relish

5 large beetroot (1kg), peeled, chopped coarsely

4 large white onions (800g), chopped coarsely

1 cup (220g) caster sugar

1 tablespoon coarse cooking salt

1 teaspoon ground allspice

2 cups (500ml) malt vinegar

1 tablespoon plain flour

Blend or process beetroot and onion, in batches, until chopped finely. Combine beetroot mixture, sugar, salt, allspice and 1½ cups (375ml) of the vinegar in large saucepan; bring to a boil. Boil, uncovered, stirring occasionally, 30 minutes.

Stir in blended flour and remaining vinegar; stir over heat until mixture boils and thickens.

Spoon hot relish into hot sterilised jars; seal while hot.

MAKES about 1.75 litres (7 cups)
Per tablespoon 0g fat; 79kJ
Storage In refrigerator for about 1 month

12 sun-dried tomato
chutney

Place tomatoes in medium heatproof bowl, cover with boiling water; stand about 5 minutes or until soft. Drain tomatoes, chop coarsely.
Heat oil in large heavy-base saucepan; cook onion, ginger, seeds and spice, stirring, until onion is soft. Add tomato and remaining ingredients; stir over heat, without boiling, until sugar dissolves. Simmer, uncovered, stirring occasionally, about 50 minutes or until mixture thickens.
Spoon hot chutney into hot sterilised jars; seal while hot.

MAKES about 1.5 litres (6 cups)
Per tablespoon 0.5g fat; 127kJ
Storage In cool, dark place for about 6 months; refrigerate after opening

3 cups (180g) dry-packed sun-dried tomatoes

1 tablespoon olive oil

2 medium white onions (300g), chopped finely

2 teaspoons grated fresh ginger

3 teaspoons black mustard seeds

2 teaspoons mixed spice

3 medium apples (450g), peeled, chopped finely

1 cup (160g) sultanas

1 cup (200g) firmly packed brown sugar

2 cups (500ml) apple juice

1 cup (250ml) balsamic vinegar

1/2 cup (125ml) cider vinegar

1/3 cup (80ml) water

1/4 cup (60ml) lemon juice

1 teaspoon coarse cooking salt

1 medium pineapple
(1.25kg), peeled,
chopped finely

2 teaspoons coarse
cooking salt

1 litre (4 cups)
malt vinegar

1 tablespoon grated
fresh ginger

2 cloves garlic,
crushed

2 medium white
onions (300g),
chopped finely

1 small red capsicum
(150g), chopped finely

1 tablespoon
tomato paste

2 cups (500ml) water

1¹/₂ cups (330g) sugar

Place pineapple in large bowl, sprinkle with salt. Cover; stand overnight.
Rinse pineapple under cold water; drain well.

Combine pineapple, vinegar, ginger, garlic, onion, capsicum, paste
and the water in large heavy-base saucepan; bring to a boil. Simmer,
uncovered, 30 minutes. Add sugar; stir over heat, without boiling, until
sugar dissolves. Simmer, uncovered, stirring occasionally, about
30 minutes or until mixture thickens.

Spoon hot relish into hot sterilised jars; seal while hot.

MAKES about 1 litre (4 cups)
Per tablespoon 0g fat; 156kJ
Storage In refrigerator for about 1 month

14 rhubarb and
tomato chutney

You will need 1 bunch rhubarb (700g) for this recipe.

1 tablespoon olive oil

1½ tablespoons black mustard seeds

1½ tablespoons ground cumin

½ teaspoon ground cloves

1½ tablespoons ground coriander

11 medium tomatoes (2kg), chopped coarsely

2 large white onions (400g), chopped finely

1 teaspoon coarse cooking salt

2 cloves garlic, crushed

2 cups (340g) raisins

1 cup (200g) firmly packed brown sugar

1 cup (250ml) malt vinegar

4 cups chopped fresh rhubarb stems

Heat oil in large heavy-base saucepan; cook seeds and spices, stirring, until fragrant. Add tomato, onion, salt, garlic, raisins, sugar and vinegar. Stir over heat, without boiling, until sugar dissolves. Simmer, uncovered, stirring occasionally, about 35 minutes or until mixture thickens. Stir in rhubarb; simmer, uncovered, stirring occasionally, about 5 minutes or until rhubarb is tender.

Spoon hot chutney into hot sterilised jars; seal while hot.

MAKES about 2 litres (8 cups)
Per tablespoon 0.3g fat; 110kJ
Storage In cool, dark place for about 6 months; refrigerate after opening

fig, tomato and caramelised onion jam

1 tablespoon olive oil

4 medium onions (600g), sliced thinly

2 tablespoons white wine vinegar

1/4 cup (55g) sugar

6 large tomatoes (1.5kg), peeled, chopped

3 1/2 cups (700g) dried figs, sliced

1/2 cup (125ml) lemon juice

4 cups (880g) sugar, extra

Heat oil in large frying pan, add onion; cook, stirring, about 15 minutes or until onion is very soft. Add vinegar and sugar; cook, stirring often, about 20 minutes or until mixture is lightly browned.

Meanwhile, combine tomato with fig in large heavy-base saucepan. Simmer, uncovered, about 20 minutes or until fruit is pulpy.

Add onion mixture and remaining ingredients; stir over heat, without boiling, until extra sugar is dissolved. Boil, uncovered, stirring occasionally, about 20 minutes or until jam jells when tested on a cold saucer. Pour hot jam into hot sterilised jars; seal immediately.

MAKES about 1.5 litres (6 cups)
Per tablespoon 0g fat; 310kJ
Storage In cool, dark place for about 6 months; refrigerate after opening.

16 pawpaw

and chilli chutney

1/2 teaspoon black peppercorns

1/2 teaspoon whole allspice

1 large pawpaw (1.5kg), peeled, chopped coarsely

2 large apples (400g), peeled, chopped coarsely

3 small tomatoes (390g), peeled, chopped coarsely

2 cups (440g) sugar

3 cups (750ml) white vinegar

2 teaspoons coarse cooking salt

3 fresh red Thai chillies, seeded, chopped finely

2 teaspoons grated fresh ginger

Tie peppercorns and allspice in piece of muslin. Place muslin bag in large heavy-base saucepan with remaining ingredients. Stir over heat, without boiling, until sugar dissolves. Simmer, uncovered, stirring occasionally, about 1 1/2 hours or until mixture thickens. Discard bag.
Spoon hot chutney into hot sterilised jars; seal while hot.

MAKES about 1.25 litres (5 cups)
Per tablespoon 0g fat; 101kJ
Storage In cool, dark place for about 6 months; refrigerate after opening

6 medium
beetroot (1kg)

1 cup (220g) sugar

1 litre (4 cups)
cider vinegar

1 small cinnamon stick

8 black peppercorns

4 small dried chillies

1 teaspoon black
mustard seeds

Trim beetroot, leaving 3cm of the stem attached. Wash carefully.
Add beetroot to large saucepan of cold water; boil 45 minutes or until
tender. Allow to cool in the cooking water. Reserve ½ cup (125ml)
of the liquid.
Rub skin off beetroot; quarter, then place in hot sterilised jars.
Combine reserved cooking liquid, sugar, vinegar and remaining
ingredients in large saucepan; stir over heat, without boiling, until
sugar is dissolved. Bring to a boil. Pour liquid over beetroot and
seal while hot.

MAKES about 2 litres (24 pieces)
Per piece 0g fat; 232kJ
Storage In cool, dark place for about 6 months; refrigerate after opening

18 pickled chillies

1kg fresh red Thai chillies
8 dried bay leaves
1 tablespoon black peppercorns
1 tablespoon coriander seeds
2½ cups (625ml) water
¼ cup (55g) fine sea salt
1 tablespoon sugar
1½ cups (375ml) white vinegar
1½ cups (375ml) malt vinegar

Add chillies to large saucepan of boiling water; return to boil, drain. Rinse chillies under cold water; drain well. Pack chillies, bay leaves, peppercorns and seeds firmly into hot sterilised jars.
Combine the water, salt and sugar in medium saucepan; stir over heat until salt dissolves and mixture boils. Remove pan from heat, stir in vinegars.
Pour vinegar mixture over chillies in jars to cover completely; seal while hot.

MAKES about 2 litres (8 cups)
Per chilli 0.1g fat; 33kJ
Storage In cool, dark place for about 6 months; refrigerate after opening

vegetables

1 clove garlic, sliced thinly

2 tablespoons balsamic vinegar

4 medium red capsicums (800g)

16 baby eggplants (1kg)

2 teaspoons coarse cooking salt

2 cups (500ml) olive oil

½ cup (125ml) vegetable oil

2 teaspoons dried thyme leaves

2 teaspoons dried oregano leaves

Combine garlic and vinegar in small bowl; stand 30 minutes. Quarter capsicums, remove and discard seeds and membranes. Roast under grill or in very hot oven, skin-side up, until skin blisters and blackens. Cover capsicum pieces in plastic or paper for 5 minutes, peel away skin. Cut capsicum into thick pieces.

Cut eggplants lengthways into 5mm slices. Char-grill (or grill or barbecue) eggplant and capsicum, in batches, until eggplant is browned and just tender and capsicum is browned.

Pack hot vegetables into 1.5-litre (6-cup) wide-necked hot sterilised jar. Combine salt, oils, and herbs in small saucepan; stir over heat until hot. Remove from heat, carefully add vinegar and garlic. Pour oil mixture over vegetables in jar to cover completely; seal while hot. Invert jar every few days.

MAKES about 1.5 litres (6 cups)

Per vegetable piece 3.1g fat; 26kJ

Storage In refrigerator for about 1 month

20 pickled olives

*These will be ready to eat after about
5 weeks sealed in salted water; do not
mix green and black varieties of olives
when pickling them.*

1.5kg fresh black or green olives

1/3 cup (75g) fine sea salt

1 litre (4 cups) water

1/2 cup (125ml) olive oil

Discard any over-blemished olives. Using
a sharp knife, make two cuts lengthways
in each olive, through to stone.
Place olives in 2-litre (8-cup) sterilised
jars until jars are two-thirds full; cover
olives with cold water. To keep olives
submerged, fill a small plastic bag with
cold water, tie bag securely, sit on top
of olives in jar. Scum will appear on
surface of water. Change water in jars
daily, refilling with fresh, cold water.
Change water for 4 days with black
olives, 6 days with green olives.
Combine sea salt and the 1 litre
(4 cups) of water in medium saucepan,
stir over heat until salt is dissolved;
cool. Discard water in jars; fill with
enough salted water to cover olives.
Pour enough oil in jars to cover
completely; seal jars.

MAKES about 2 litres
Per olive 3g fat; 29kJ
Storage In cool, dark place for about
6 months; refrigerate after opening

marinated olives 21

Olives must be pickled before they can be marinated; after being marinated 2 weeks, olives will be ready to eat.

600g drained black or green pickled olives

1 clove garlic, sliced

2 lemon wedges

1 sprig fresh dill

2 cups (500ml) olive oil

Combine olives, garlic, lemon and dill in 1-litre (4-cup) hot sterilised jar, add enough oil to cover olives; seal jar.

MAKES about 1 litre
Per olive 3.1g fat; 31kJ
Storage In cool, dark place for about 2 months; refrigerate after opening

sun-dried tomato and
olive tapenade

1 cup (150g) drained
sun-dried tomatoes
in oil

1 tablespoon olive oil

1 tablespoon red
wine vinegar

1 tablespoon
brown sugar

1 tablespoon chopped
fresh oregano leaves

1 tablespoon chopped
fresh basil leaves

$1/2$ teaspoon cracked
black peppercorns

$2/3$ cup (70g)
pecans, toasted

$1/3$ cup (50g) seeded
black olives

Process ingredients
until smooth. Spoon
tapenade into cold
sterilised jars;
seal immediately.

MAKES about
2 cups (500ml)
Per tablespoon
4.7g fat; 246kJ
Storage In refrigerator
for about 6 weeks

fiery chilli

tomato chutney

8 medium tomatoes (1.5kg), peeled, seeded, chopped coarsely

1 large white onion (200g), chopped finely

4 cloves garlic, crushed

1 medium red capsicum (200g), chopped finely

2 teaspoons grated fresh ginger

2 cups (500ml) cider vinegar

2 cups (440g) sugar

1/2 cup (125ml) lemon juice

1 cup (160g) sultanas

2 teaspoons coarse cooking salt

1 cinnamon stick

6 whole cloves

5 red Thai chillies, seeded, chopped finely

2 teaspoons chilli powder

Combine tomato, onion, garlic, capsicum and ginger in large heavy-base saucepan; bring to a boil. Simmer, uncovered, stirring occasionally, about 15 minutes or until onion is soft.
Add remaining ingredients; stir over heat, without boiling, until sugar dissolves. Simmer, uncovered, stirring occasionally, about 1 hour or until mixture thickens. Discard cinnamon stick.
Spoon hot chutney into hot sterilised jars; seal while hot.

MAKES about 1.5 litres (6 cups)
Per tablespoon 0.1g fat; 145kJ
Storage In cool, dark place for about 6 months; refrigerate after opening

24 piccalilli

Combine cauliflower, carrot, celery, tomato, cucumber, onion and salt in large bowl. Cover; stand overnight.

Rinse vegetables under cold water; drain well. Combine vinegar, sugar, turmeric, mustard powder, ginger, garlic and chilli in large saucepan; bring to a boil. Add vegetables; simmer, covered, about 5 minutes or until vegetables are just tender. Stir in blended cornflour and extra vinegar; stir over heat until mixture boils and thickens.

Spoon hot Piccalilli into hot sterilised jars; seal while hot.

MAKES about 3 litres (12 cups)
Per tablespoon 0g fat; 45kJ
Storage In refrigerator for about 1 month

$^{1}/_{2}$ small cauliflower (350g), chopped coarsely

2 medium carrots (240g), sliced thinly

2 trimmed celery sticks (150g), sliced thickly

2 small green tomatoes (260g), chopped coarsely

1 large green cucumber (400g), sliced thickly

10 baby brown onions (250g), quartered

1 cup (260g) coarse cooking salt

1.25 litres (5 cups) white vinegar

1 cup (220g) sugar

1 tablespoon ground turmeric

1 tablespoon mustard powder

$^{1}/_{2}$ teaspoon ground ginger

2 cloves garlic, crushed

2 red Thai chillies, seeded, chopped finely

$^{1}/_{4}$ cup (35g) cornflour

$^{1}/_{4}$ cup (60ml) white vinegar, extra

mint relish

1 cup (250ml)
cider vinegar

1/2 cup (110g) raw sugar

1/2 teaspoon mild
curry powder

1/2 teaspoon
mustard powder

4 Lebanese cucumbers
(520g), peeled,
chopped finely

4 small tomatoes (520g),
chopped finely

1/2 cup (85g) raisins

1 cup finely chopped
fresh mint leaves

Combine vinegar, sugar,
curry powder and
mustard powder in large
saucepan; stir over
heat, without boiling,
until sugar dissolves.
Bring to a boil. Remove
pan from heat; stir in
remaining ingredients.
Spoon hot relish into
hot sterilised jars; seal
while hot.

MAKES about
1 litre (4 cups)
Per tablespoon
0.1g fat; 72kJ
Storage In refrigerator
for about 1 month

26 pickled capsicums

13 small red
capsicums (2kg)

1 litre (4 cups)
white vinegar

1 tablespoon black
peppercorns

6 sprigs fresh parsley

3 sprigs fresh thyme

2 bay leaves

Cut capsicums in quarters lengthways, remove seeds. Place capsicum, skin-side up, under hot grill. Grill until skin blisters, cool slightly; remove skin. Pack capsicum into hot sterilised jars.
Combine vinegar, peppercorns and herbs in medium saucepan; bring to a boil. Simmer, uncovered, 5 minutes; strain. Pour hot vinegar over capsicum to cover; seal when cold.

MAKES 52 pieces
Per piece 0g fat; 10kJ
Storage In cool, dry place for up to 6 months; refrigerate after opening

mushrooms with **bite**

These are great as an appetiser or served alongside mature cheddar cheese, as in a ploughman's lunch.

3 cups (750ml) cider vinegar

¹/₂ cup (125ml) lemon juice

10 whole white peppercorns

2 fresh bay leaves

2 sprigs fresh thyme

2 cloves garlic, sliced thinly

3 small fresh red Thai chillies, seeded

1kg button mushrooms

Combine all ingredients except mushrooms in large saucepan. Bring to a boil, reduce heat; simmer, covered, 10 minutes. Add mushrooms; simmer, uncovered, 10 minutes. Pour mixture into hot sterilised jars; seal while hot.

SERVES 4
Per serving 0.9g fat; 399kJ
Storage In cool, dry place for up to 6 months; refrigerate after opening

28 cauliflower and
capsicum pickles

1 small cauliflower (700g), chopped coarsely

2 medium white onions (300g), chopped coarsely

1 medium red capsicum (200g), chopped coarsely

1 tablespoon coarse cooking salt

1 cup (250ml) white vinegar

1/2 cup (110g) sugar

1/2 teaspoon ground allspice

2 cloves

1 dried bay leaf

1 tablespoon mild curry powder

1 tablespoon mustard powder

1 tablespoon seeded mustard

1 teaspoon ground turmeric

1 tablespoon plain flour

1/4 cup (60ml) white vinegar, extra

Place cauliflower, onion and capsicum in large bowl, sprinkle with salt. Cover; stand overnight. **Rinse** vegetables under cold water; drain well. Combine vinegar, sugar, allspice, cloves and bay leaf in large saucepan; bring to a boil. Add vegetables; simmer, covered, about 20 minutes or until vegetables are just tender.
Stir in blended curry powder, mustards, turmeric, flour and extra vinegar; stir over heat until mixture boils and thickens. Spoon hot pickles into hot sterilised jars; seal while hot.

MAKES about 1 litre (4 cups)
Per tablespoon 0.2g fat; 97kJ
Storage In refrigerator for about 1 month

spicy pickled onions

80 baby brown onions (2kg)

3 cups (780g) coarse cooking salt

1.25 litres (5 cups) white vinegar

1 tablespoon coarse cooking salt, extra

1 tablespoon sugar

1½ teaspoons cloves

2 teaspoons allspice

2 teaspoons black peppercorns

Place unpeeled onions and salt in large bowl, add enough water to just float the onions. Cover; stand 2 days, stirring occasionally. Drain onions, discard liquid. Peel onions carefully, leaving ends intact.

Place onions in large heatproof bowl. Cover with boiling water, stand 3 minutes; drain. Repeat this process twice. Pack hot onions firmly into hot sterilised jars.

Bring remaining ingredients to a boil in medium saucepan; simmer, uncovered, 15 minutes. Pour hot vinegar mixture over onions in jars to cover completely; seal while hot.

MAKES 80
Per onion 0g fat; 80kJ
Storage In cool, dark place for about 6 months; refrigerate after opening

30 preserved lemons

6 small lemons (700g)

2 tablespoons coarse cooking salt

1 cinnamon stick

1 teaspoon cardamom seeds

1 teaspoon black peppercorns

1 teaspoon yellow mustard seeds

1 dried bay leaf

2 cups (500ml) lemon juice, approximately

Quarter lemons lengthways to within 5mm of the base. Open out lemons, sprinkle cut surfaces with salt; reshape lemons.

Pack lemons firmly into 1-litre (4-cup) hot sterilised jar, add spices and bay leaf. Pour lemon juice over lemons in jars to cover completely. To keep lemons submerged, fill a small plastic bag with cold water, tie bag securely, sit on top of lemons in jar. Seal jar.

Store in cool, dark place, shaking and turning jar every 2 days. Stand 4 weeks before using.

To serve lemons, remove and discard flesh from rind. Squeeze out excess liquid from rind, rinse rind well and slice thinly.

MAKES 24 pieces
Per piece 0g fat; 53kJ
Storage In cool, dark place for about 6 months; refrigerate after opening

If you've made every pickle, relish and chutney recipe known to man and you still have a glut of unused produce, it's time you tried something different.

oven-dried tomatoes in basil oil

30 small egg tomatoes (1.8kg)

4 cloves garlic, sliced thinly

12 fresh basil leaves

2 tablespoons fine sea salt

2 cups (500ml) olive oil

Cut tomatoes in half lengthways. Place garlic, basil and tomatoes, cut-side up, on wire racks over oven trays. Sprinkle tomatoes with salt. Dry in very slow oven 6 to 8 hours or until tomatoes are dry to touch. Basil will take about 20 minutes to dry, garlic about 30 minutes; remove basil and garlic from oven, separately, when each is crisp. Turn and rearrange tomatoes several times during drying. Pack tomatoes, garlic and basil into 1-litre (4-cup) hot sterilised jar.

Pour oil over tomatoes in jar to cover completely; seal immediately.

For semi-dried tomatoes: Follow above method, but only dry tomatoes for about 3 hours or until tomatoes are semi-dried.

Per half-tomato 3g fat; 30kJ
Storage Oven-dried and semi-dried tomatoes will keep in the refrigerator for about 1 month

Placing tomatoes on rack

Rearranging tomatoes

Pouring oil over tomatoes

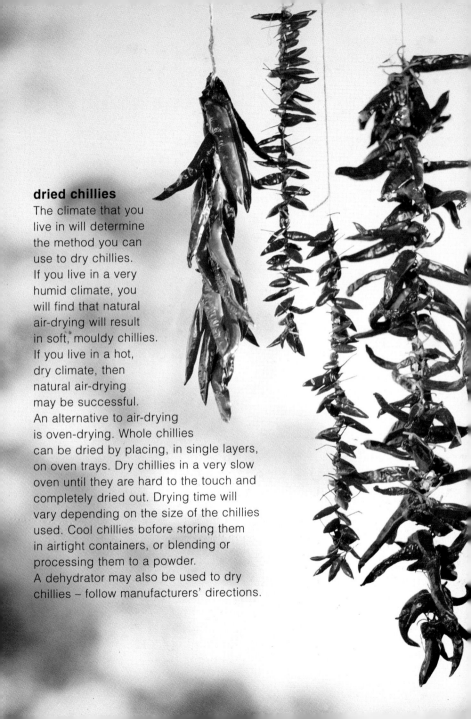

dried chillies

The climate that you
live in will determine
the method you can
use to dry chillies.
If you live in a very
humid climate, you
will find that natural
air-drying will result
in soft, mouldy chillies.
If you live in a hot,
dry climate, then
natural air-drying
may be successful.
An alternative to air-drying
is oven-drying. Whole chillies
can be dried by placing, in single layers,
on oven trays. Dry chillies in a very slow
oven until they are hard to the touch and
completely dried out. Drying time will
vary depending on the size of the chillies
used. Cool chillies before storing them
in airtight containers, or blending or
processing them to a powder.
A dehydrator may also be used to dry
chillies – follow manufacturers' directions.

34 pear and walnut chutney

9 small pears
(1.6kg), peeled,
chopped coarsely

2 large apples
(400g), peeled,
chopped coarsely

1 cup (250ml)
white vinegar

3/4 cup (180ml)
lemon juice

1 cup (200g) firmly
packed brown sugar

1 cup (170g) coarsely
chopped raisins

1 cup (160g) coarsely
chopped seeded dates

1 cup (120g) coarsely
chopped walnuts

Combine ingredients in large heavy-base
saucepan; bring to a boil. Simmer, uncovered,
stirring occasionally, about 1¼ hours or until
mixture thickens.

Spoon hot chutney into hot sterilised jars;
seal while hot.

MAKES about 1.25 litres (5 cups)
Per tablespoon 1.5g fat; 234kJ
Storage In cool, dark place for about 6 months;
refrigerate after opening

fig and

apple chutney

10 medium figs
(600g), chopped
coarsely

1 large white onion
(200g), chopped finely

3 medium apples
(450g), peeled,
chopped finely

2 cups (400g) firmly
packed brown sugar

1 cup (160g) sultanas

1/2 cup (75g) finely
chopped dried apricots

2 cups (500ml)
white vinegar

1 cup (250ml)
dry white wine

1/4 cup (60ml)
tomato paste

1 tablespoon yellow
mustard seeds

1 clove garlic, crushed

1/2 teaspoon
ground cinnamon

1/2 teaspoon
ground cardamom

Combine ingredients in large heavy-base
saucepan; stir over heat, without boiling,
until sugar dissolves. Simmer, uncovered,
stirring occasionally, about 1 1/2 hours or
until mixture thickens.
Spoon hot chutney into hot sterilised jars;
seal while hot.

MAKES about 1.5 litres (6 cups)
Per tablespoon 0.1g fat; 169kJ
Storage In cool, dark place for about 6 months;
refrigerate after opening

36 barbecue

sauce

2 tablespoons
vegetable oil

2 medium brown
onions (300g),
chopped finely

3 cloves garlic,
crushed

1/2 cup (125ml)
treacle

1/3 cup (90g)
Dijon mustard

1/3 cup (80ml)
Worcestershire
sauce

800g can
tomatoes

1/2 cup (125g)
tomato paste

1 cup (250ml)
water

1 tablespoon
cornflour

2 tablespoons
water, extra

Heat oil in large saucepan; cook
onion, stirring, until very soft.
Add garlic, treacle, mustard, sauce,
undrained crushed tomatoes, paste
and the water; bring to a boil. Simmer,
uncovered, stirring occasionally,
about 20 minutes or until mixture
thickens. Stir in blended cornflour
and extra water; stir over heat until
mixture boils and thickens.
Blend or process sauce until smooth;
push through sieve. Pour hot sauce
into hot sterilised jars; seal while hot.

MAKES about 1.5 litres (6 cups)
Per tablespoon 0.6g fat; 74kJ
Storage In refrigerator for about 2 weeks

tomato and 37
choko chutney

2 x 800g cans diced tomatoes

2 large chokoes (700g), peeled, cored, chopped finely

2 medium brown onions (300g), chopped finely

1½ cups (375ml) malt vinegar

2 cups (400g) firmly packed brown sugar

2 tablespoons mustard powder

1 tablespoon mild curry paste

2 cloves garlic, crushed

1 teaspoon ground allspice

2 teaspoons coarse cooking salt

¼ teaspoon ground black pepper

1 tablespoon cornflour

¼ cup (60ml) malt vinegar, extra

Combine undrained tomatoes, chokoes, onion, vinegar, sugar, half of the mustard powder, curry paste, garlic, allspice, salt and pepper in large saucepan. Stir over heat, without boiling, until sugar dissolves. Simmer, uncovered, stirring occasionally, about 1½ hours or until mixture thickens.

Stir in blended cornflour, extra vinegar and remaining mustard powder; stir over heat until mixture boils and thickens.

Spoon hot chutney into hot sterilised jars; seal while hot.

MAKES about 2.25 litres (9 cups)
Per tablespoon 0.1g fat; 86kJ
Storage In cool, dark place for about 6 months; refrigerate after opening

38 banana and
coconut relish

Combine mustard seeds and vinegar in small bowl, cover; stand overnight.
Combine coconut with the water and extra vinegar in medium bowl, cover; stand 1 hour.
Heat oil in large heavy-base saucepan; cook onion, garlic, ginger, chilli, chilli powder, cumin and turmeric, stirring, until fragrant. Add tomato; cook, stirring, until tomato is soft. Stir in mustard seed mixture and bananas; simmer, uncovered, stirring occasionally, until mixture thickens. Stir in sugar, then coconut mixture; simmer, uncovered, stirring occasionally, about 10 minutes or until mixture thickens. Stir in remaining ingredients.
Spoon hot relish into hot sterilised jars; seal while hot.

MAKES about 1.75 litres (7 cups)
Per tablespoon 4.3g fat; 233kJ
Storage In refrigerator for about 1 month

1 tablespoon black mustard seeds

1/4 cup (60ml) white vinegar

1 1/2 cups (105g) shredded coconut

1 cup (250ml) water

3/4 cup (180ml) white vinegar, extra

1 1/4 cups (310ml) vegetable oil

1 small brown onion (80g), chopped finely

2 cloves garlic, crushed

3 teaspoons grated fresh ginger

12 fresh red Thai chillies, seeded, chopped finely

2 teaspoons chilli powder

1 tablespoon ground cumin

2 tablespoons ground turmeric

2 small tomatoes (260g), chopped coarsely

6 medium ripe bananas (1.2kg), chopped coarsely

3/4 cup (150g) firmly packed brown sugar

3 teaspoons coarse cooking salt

1 tablespoon lime juice

1/4 cup chopped fresh coriander leaves

mango and

port chutney

4 medium mangoes
(1.7kg), peeled,
chopped coarsely

3/4 cup (180ml) port

2 large white onions
(400g), chopped finely

1 cup (170g) coarsely
chopped raisins

2 teaspoons grated
fresh ginger

2 fresh red Thai
chillies, chopped finely

2 cups (440g) sugar

3 cups (750ml)
malt vinegar

2 teaspoons yellow
mustard seeds

Combine ingredients in large heavy-base
saucepan; stir over heat, without boiling,
until sugar dissolves. Simmer, uncovered,
stirring occasionally, about 1 1/2 hours, or
until mixture thickens.

Spoon hot chutney into hot sterilised jars;
seal while hot.

MAKES about 1.25 litres (5 cups)
Per tablespoon 0.1g fat; 235kJ
Storage In cool, dark place for about 6 months;
refrigerate after opening

40 peach and
lemon chutney

8 black peppercorns

4 small dried red chillies

2 cloves

1 cinnamon stick

5 medium peaches (750g), peeled, seeded, chopped coarsely

2 large white onions (400g), chopped finely

2 cups (400g) firmly packed brown sugar

2 cups (500ml) malt vinegar

1 cup (160g) sultanas

3 teaspoons grated fresh ginger

2 cloves garlic, crushed

2 teaspoons finely grated lemon rind

1/4 cup (60ml) lemon juice

Tie peppercorns, chillies, cloves and cinnamon in a piece of muslin. Place muslin bag in large heavy-base saucepan with remaining ingredients; stir over heat, without boiling, until sugar dissolves. Simmer, uncovered, stirring occasionally, about 1 1/2 hours or until mixture thickens. Discard bag.

Spoon hot chutney into hot sterilised jars; seal while hot.

MAKES about 1 litre (4 cups)

Per tablespoon 0g fat; 209kJ

Storage In cool, dark place for about 6 months; refrigerate after opening

plum chutney

60g butter

2 cloves garlic, crushed

2 teaspoons grated fresh ginger

2 teaspoons ground cumin

1 teaspoon ground cardamom

2 teaspoons yellow mustard seeds

2 medium onions (300g), sliced

14 medium plums (1kg),
pitted, chopped

2 large apples (400g),
peeled, chopped

2 cups (400g) firmly packed
brown sugar

1 cup (250ml) dry red wine

2 cups (500ml) white vinegar

Heat butter in large saucepan, add
garlic and ginger, cook 1 minute.
Stir in spices, seeds and onion;
cook until onion is soft. Stir in
remaining ingredients, stir over
heat, without boiling, until sugar is
dissolved. Bring to a boil; simmer,
uncovered, stirring occasionally, for
about 1½ hours or until thick. Pour
into hot sterilised jars; seal when cold.

MAKES about 1.5 litres (6 cups)
Per tablespoon 0.7g fat; 156kJ
Storage In cool, dark place for about
6 months; refrigerate after opening

42 banana-chilli pickle

3kg banana chillies

8 fresh red Thai chillies

³/₄ cup (250g) coarse cooking salt

2 tablespoons dill seeds

³/₄ cup (75g) aniseed

²/₃ cup (120g) yellow mustard seeds

2 tablespoons black mustard seeds

2 tablespoons fennel seeds

1 cup (250ml) peanut oil

Roughly blend or process chillies, place in large bowl, stir through salt; stand 2 hours.

Meanwhile, heat large frying pan; dry-fry seeds, one variety at a time, until fragrant.

Heat oil to smoking point; cool. Pour liquid off chillies; squeeze the mixture, wearing kitchen gloves, to remove as much moisture as possible.

Combine chillies, oil and seeds, mix well; pour into jars, seal. Keep in cool, dark place 3 months before using.

MAKES 2 litres (8 cups)
Per tablespoon 2.7g fat; 128kJ
Storage In cool, dark place for about 6 months; refrigerate after opening

7 medium apples (1kg)

1.5 litres
(6 cups) water

1/3 cup (80ml)
lemon juice

1/3 cup coarsely
chopped fresh
mint leaves

3 cups (660g) sugar,
approximately

2 tablespoons finely
chopped fresh mint
leaves, extra

Chop unpeeled apples; do not discard seeds. Combine apple, seeds, the water, juice and mint in large heavy-base saucepan; bring to a boil. Simmer, covered, about 40 minutes or until apple is very soft. Strain mixture through a fine cloth into a large heatproof bowl. Allow liquid to drip through cloth slowly; do not squeeze or press pulp as this will make a cloudy jelly; discard pulp.

Measure apple liquid, pour into a large clean, heavy-base saucepan. Add 3/4 cup (165g) sugar to each 1 cup (250ml) liquid (mixture should not be more than 5cm deep at this stage). Stir over heat, without boiling, until sugar dissolves. Boil, uncovered, without stirring, about 30 minutes or until jelly sets when tested on a cold saucer. Remove from heat; stand for 5 minutes. Stir in extra mint.

Pour hot jelly into hot sterilised jars; seal while hot.

MAKES about 3 cups (750ml)
Per tablespoon 0g fat; 348kJ
Storage In refrigerator for about 2 months

44 mixed fruit chutney

1 teaspoon cloves

1 teaspoon black peppercorns

3/4 cup (110g) dried apricots, chopped coarsely

3/4 cup (125g) seeded dates, chopped coarsely

4 large apples (800g), peeled, chopped coarsely

2 large white onions (400g), chopped finely

1 teaspoon grated fresh ginger

2 teaspoons coarse cooking salt

1 cup (200g) firmly packed brown sugar

2 1/2 cups (625ml) malt vinegar

Tie cloves and peppercorns in piece of muslin.

Place apricots in medium bowl, cover with hot water; stand 30 minutes. Drain apricots, combine in large heavy-base saucepan with muslin bag, dates, apple, onion, ginger, salt, sugar and vinegar. Stir over heat, without boiling, until sugar dissolves. Simmer, uncovered, stirring occasionally, about 45 minutes or until mixture thickens. Discard bag.

Spoon hot chutney into hot sterilised jars; seal while hot.

MAKES about 1.25 litres (5 cups)
Per tablespoon 0g fat; 125kJ
Storage In cool, dark place for about 6 months: refrigerate after opening

chilli apple chutney

2 fresh red Thai chillies, seeded, chopped finely

10 large apples (2kg), peeled, chopped coarsely

1 clove garlic, crushed

2¼ cups (375g) raisins, chopped coarsely

½ cup (115g) glacé ginger, chopped finely

5 cups (1kg) firmly packed brown sugar

1 litre (4 cups) white vinegar

1 tablespoon coarse cooking salt

1 tablespoon mixed spice

2 teaspoons five-spice powder

1 tablespoon ground turmeric

2 bay leaves

Combine ingredients in large heavy-base saucepan; stir over heat, without boiling, until sugar dissolves. Simmer, uncovered, stirring occasionally, about 2 hours or until mixture thickens. Discard bay leaves.
Spoon hot chutney into hot sterilised jars; seal while hot.

MAKES about 1.75 litres (7 cups)
Per tablespoon 0.1g fat; 301kJ
Storage In cool, dark place for about 6 months; refrigerate after opening

46 eggplant pickle

Wash eggplants; cut into 2cm cubes. Place eggplant in colander in sink, stir in combined salt and turmeric; stand 1 hour. Pat eggplant cubes dry with absorbent paper.

Heat oil in large frying pan; cook eggplant, in batches, until soft. Drain cooked eggplant on absorbent paper. Reserve used oil.

Blend or process seeds and vinegar, then add garlic, ginger and onion; blend until smooth.

In heated small frying pan, dry-fry ground spices until fragrant.

Heat ³/₄ cup reserved oil in large saucepan, add eggplant, vinegar mixture, spice mixture, tamarind, chilli and cinnamon; simmer, covered, 20 minutes. Stir in sugar.

Remove cinnamon stick, place mixture into jar; seal while hot.

MAKES 1.25 litres (5 cups)
Per tablespoon 6.1g fat; 264kJ
Storage In cool, dry place for up to 6 months; refrigerate after opening

If you prefer, 4 small eggplants or 16 baby eggplants can be used in place of the eggplants below.

2 large (1kg) eggplants

2 teaspoons salt

2 teaspoons ground turmeric

2 cups (500ml) vegetable oil

1 tablespoon black mustard seeds

¹/₂ cup (125ml) brown vinegar

5 cloves garlic, crushed

2 tablespoons grated fresh ginger

1 large brown onion (200g), chopped

1 teaspoon ground fennel

2 teaspoons ground cumin

1 tablespoon ground coriander

4 tablespoons tamarind concentrate

2 teaspoons dried chilli flakes

1 cinnamon stick

2 teaspoons palm sugar

8 large tomatoes
(2kg), cored

2/3 cup (160ml)
olive oil

10 cloves garlic,
peeled

1 tablespoon grated
fresh ginger

10 small fresh
red Thai chillies,
stems removed

2 tablespoons
cumin seeds

2 tablespoons black
mustard seeds

3/4 cup (180ml) red
wine vinegar

1/4 cup (60ml)
fish sauce

1 1/4 cups (335g) palm
sugar, chopped

1 tablespoon
ground turmeric

1/2 cup chopped fresh
coriander leaves
and roots

Rub tomatoes with olive oil; place in a roasting
pan and cook in a moderate oven for about
30 minutes or until soft, but not coloured.
Blend or process garlic, ginger, chillies and
seeds until chopped and well combined. Transfer
mixture to large heavy-base saucepan, add
tomato, vinegar, fish sauce, sugar and turmeric;
simmer, uncovered, about 2 hours or until thick.
Blend or process, in batches, until combined
but still textured. Return to heat for 5 minutes
or until hot; stir in coriander. Spoon into hot
sterilised jars; seal while hot.

MAKES about 1.5 litres (6 cups)
Per tablespoon 2.2g fat; 176kJ
Storage In cool, dry place for up to 6 months;
refrigerate after opening

tomato, eggplant and
capsicum relish

2 small eggplants (460g)

1 tablespoon coarse cooking salt

3 medium red capsicums (600g)

2 tablespoons olive oil

1 large white onion (200g), sliced thinly

1 clove garlic, crushed

2 teaspoons black mustard seeds

3 teaspoons cumin seeds

1/4 teaspoon cardamom seeds

6 medium tomatoes (1.1kg), peeled, seeded, chopped coarsely

3/4 cup (180ml) white wine vinegar

1/4 cup (60ml) red wine vinegar

1 tablespoon balsamic vinegar

1/3 cup (75g) firmly packed brown sugar

Cut eggplants into 2cm slices; place on wire rack, sprinkle with salt. Stand 10 minutes. Rinse slices under cold water; drain on absorbent paper. Chop eggplant slices coarsely.

Quarter capsicums, remove and discard seeds and membranes. Roast under grill or in very hot oven, skin-side up, until skin blisters and blackens. Cover capsicum pieces with plastic or paper for 5 minutes, peel away skin. Chop capsicum coarsely.

Heat oil in large heavy-base saucepan; cook onion, garlic and seeds, stirring, until onion is soft. Add eggplant; cook, stirring, until eggplant is browned lightly. Add capsicum and remaining ingredients; simmer, covered, stirring occasionally, 50 minutes. Remove lid; simmer about 10 minutes or until mixture thickens.

Spoon hot relish into hot sterilised jars; seal while hot.

MAKES about 1 litre (4 cups)
Per tablespoon 0.9g fat; 88kJ
Storage In refrigerator for about 1 month

green tomato and
pear chutney

4 small under-ripe pears
(720g), peeled, chopped

7 medium under-ripe tomatoes
(1.3kg), chopped

2 large brown onions
(400g), chopped

1 cup (150g) dried currants

1/4 cup (45g) black
mustard seeds

2 cups (500ml) brown vinegar

2 cups (400g) firmly packed
brown sugar

2 teaspoons salt

1 tablespoon ground coriander

1 tablespoon ground ginger

2 teaspoons ground cardamom

Combine ingredients in large
saucepan, stir over heat,
without boiling, until sugar is
dissolved. Simmer, uncovered,
stirring occasionally, about
1 hour or until thick. Spoon
hot chutney into hot sterilised
jars; seal immediately.

MAKES about 1.75 litres (7 cups)
Per tablespoon 0.1g fat; 133kJ
Storage In cool, dark place for
about 6 months; refrigerate
after opening

50 lime pickle with

lemon grass

10 medium limes
(800g), sliced thickly

2 teaspoons coarse
cooking salt

1 cup (250ml)
vegetable oil

4 small fresh
green Thai chillies,
chopped finely

2 teaspoons
chilli powder

1 tablespoon grated
fresh ginger

6 cloves garlic,
crushed

1 tablespoon finely
chopped fresh
lemon grass

1 teaspoon yellow
mustard seeds

2 cups (500ml)
white vinegar

Combine limes and salt in large bowl, cover;
stand overnight. Rinse lime slices under
cold water; drain.
Heat oil in large heavy-base saucepan;
cook chilli, chilli powder, ginger, garlic,
lemon grass and mustard seeds, stirring,
2 minutes. Add lime slices and vinegar; bring
to a boil. Simmer, uncovered, 10 minutes.
Spoon hot pickle into hot sterilised jars;
seal while hot. Store a week before using.

MAKES about 1.25 litres (5 cups)
Per tablespoon 3.9g fat; 163kJ
Storage In refrigerator for about 1 month

capsicum chutney

2 teaspoons black peppercorns

1 teaspoon cloves

2 large apples (400g), peeled, chopped finely

3 medium red capsicums (600g), chopped finely

2 medium white onions (300g), chopped finely

2 cloves garlic, crushed

1/2 cup (75g) dried currants

2 cups (500ml) cider vinegar

1/2 cup (125ml) dry white wine

2 1/2 cups (625ml) water

1 1/2 cups (300g) firmly packed brown sugar

Tie peppercorns and cloves in piece of muslin. Place muslin bag in large heavy-base saucepan with apple, capsicum, onion, garlic, currants, vinegar, wine and the water; bring to a boil. Simmer, uncovered, stirring occasionally, about 15 minutes or until apple and capsicum are soft.

Add sugar; stir over heat, without boiling, until sugar dissolves. Simmer, uncovered, stirring occasionally, about 1 1/2 hours or until mixture thickens. Discard bag.

Spoon hot chutney into hot sterilised jars; seal while hot.

MAKES about 3 cups (750ml)
Per tablespoon 0.1g fat; 214kJ
Storage In cool, dark place for about 6 months; refrigerate after opening

52 corn relish

3 x 440g cans corn kernels, drained

3 small brown onions
(240g), chopped

1 small red capsicum
(150g), chopped

1 small green capsicum
(150g), chopped

2 sticks celery (150g), chopped

2 cups (500ml) cider vinegar

1¾ cups (430ml) white vinegar

1 cup (220g) sugar

1 tablespoon mustard powder

1 tablespoon yellow mustard seeds

1 teaspoon ground turmeric

½ teaspoon ground cloves

¼ cup cornflour

¼ cup (60ml) white vinegar, extra

Combine corn, onion, capsicums,
celery, vinegars, sugar, mustard,
seeds, turmeric and cloves in large
saucepan. Bring to a boil; simmer,
uncovered, about 45 minutes,
stirring occasionally, or until mixture
thickens slightly. Stir in blended
cornflour and extra vinegar, stir
until mixture boils and thickens.
Pour into hot sterilised jars;
seal when cold.

MAKES about 1.5 litres (6 cups)
Per tablespoon 0g fat; 129kJ
Storage In refrigerator for up to 1 month

5 medium green tomatoes
(1kg), sliced

1 medium brown onion (150g), sliced

1kg gherkin cucumbers, chopped

1 small green capsicum
(150g), chopped

1/2 cup coarse cooking salt

2 cups (500ml) cider vinegar

1 cup (250ml) white vinegar

1 teaspoon mustard powder

1/2 teaspoon ground allspice

1/4 teaspoon mixed spice

1/4 teaspoon ground cinnamon

1/4 teaspoon ground black pepper

1 cup (200g) firmly packed brown sugar

Combine vegetables in large bowl, sprinkle with salt, cover; stand several hours. Rinse under cold water; drain well.

Combine vegetables, vinegars and spices in large saucepan. Bring to a boil; simmer, uncovered, stirring occasionally, about 45 minutes or until vegetables are pulpy. Add sugar; stir over heat, without boiling, until sugar is dissolved. Bring to a boil; boil, uncovered, 15 minutes. Pour into hot sterilised jars; seal when cold.

MAKES about 1.25 litres (5 cups)
Per tablespoon 0g fat; 29kJ
Storage In refrigerator for up to 1 month

15 Lebanese cucumbers (2kg)

¹/₃ cup (85g) coarse cooking salt

1.5 litres (6 cups) white vinegar

1 cup (220g) sugar

3 fresh red Thai chillies

2 tablespoons yellow mustard seeds

2 tablespoons black mustard seeds

1 tablespoon black peppercorns

1 tablespoon dill seeds

6 cloves

Cut cucumbers in quarters lengthways. Place cucumbers in large bowl, sprinkle with salt, cover; stand overnight. Rinse cucumbers under cold water; drain well.

Combine remaining ingredients in large saucepan; bring to a boil. Simmer, uncovered, 5 minutes. Add cucumbers; return to the boil. Pack cucumbers firmly into hot sterilised jars. Pour hot vinegar mixture over cucumbers in jars to cover completely; seal while hot.

MAKES 60 pieces
Per piece 0.1g fat; 100kJ
Storage In cool, dark place for about 6 months; refrigerate after opening

ginger mango chutney

7 large under-ripe mangoes (4.2kg), chopped coarsely

2 cups (340g) raisins

2 tablespoons grated fresh ginger

2 teaspoons coarse cooking salt

4 cloves garlic, crushed

1 fresh red Thai chilli, chopped finely

1½ cups (375ml) malt vinegar

5½ cups (1.2kg) sugar

Combine ingredients in large heavy-base saucepan; stir over heat, without boiling, until sugar dissolves. Simmer, covered, 10 minutes. Remove lid; simmer about 20 minutes or until mixture thickens.

Spoon hot chutney into hot sterilised jars; seal while hot.

MAKES about 1.5 litres (6 cups)
Per tablespoon 0.1g fat; 430kJ
Storage In cool, dark place for about 6 months; refrigerate after opening

*Below you'll find two methods
for bottling tomatoes; both are
good. Use bottled tomatoes
similarly to canned tomatoes.*

oven method

16 large egg tomatoes
(1.5kg), peeled

3 cups (750ml)
tomato juice

1/2 teaspoon coarse cooking salt

1 teaspoon sugar

Pack tomatoes into two hot
sterilised preserving jars
(each 1 litre/4 cups), fitted
with rubber rings.
Combine juice, salt and sugar
in small saucepan; bring to a
boil. Slowly pour boiling juice
over tomatoes until jars are
filled to within 1cm of top;
seal immediately with lids and
clips. Place jars, not touching,
in baking dish, add enough
boiling water to come 3cm
up sides of jars.
Stand in very slow oven
1 hour. Remove jars carefully
from dish; cool. Stand 36 hours
before removing clips.

MAKES about 2 litres (8 cups)
Per tablespoon 0g fat; 16kJ
Storage In cool, dark place for up to
6 months; refrigerate after opening

preserving unit

First check the manufacturer's guide to your preserving unit. This recipe was tested in a Fowlers Vacola year rounder food preserver, without a thermostat.

16 large egg tomatoes (1.5kg), peeled, halved

2 tablespoons lemon juice

2 cups (500ml) hot water

1 tablespoon sugar

1 teaspoon coarse cooking salt

Pack tomato into two hot sterilised preserving jars (each 1 litre/4 cups), fitted with rubber rings. Add 1 tablespoon juice to each jar. Combine remaining ingredients in medium jug, stir until sugar dissolves. Pour over the tomatoes to within 1cm of tops of jars; seal with lids and clips.
Place jars, not touching, into preserving unit, add enough cold water to come 1cm over tops of jars. Process 1 hour. Remove jars carefully from unit; cool. Stand 36 hours before removing clips.

MAKES about 2 litres (8 cups)
Per tablespoon 0g fat; 11kJ
Storage In cool, dark place for up to 6 months; refrigerate after opening

58 marinated
eggplant

10 baby eggplants (600g)

coarse cooking salt

1 litre (4 cups) white vinegar

2 cups (500ml) water

1 tablespoon chopped fresh mint

1 teaspoon dried thyme leaves

1 clove garlic, sliced finely

1 small fresh red Thai chilli,
seeded, chopped

1/2 teaspoon ground black pepper

1 1/2 cups (375ml) hot olive oil

Cut eggplants into quarters lengthways,
place eggplant in colander, sprinkle with
salt; stand 1 hour. Rinse eggplant under
cold water; drain on absorbent paper.

Heat vinegar, the water and 2 teaspoons of
salt in large saucepan until hot; do not boil.
Add eggplant; simmer gently, uncovered,
5 minutes, drain. Discard vinegar mixture.

Combine herbs, garlic, chilli, pepper and
hot oil in heatproof bowl. Place eggplant
upright in sterilised jar (1 litre/4 cup),
carefully top with enough oil mixture to
cover eggplant, leaving 1cm space between
eggplant and top of jar. Seal while hot.

MAKES 40 pieces
Per piece 2.8g fat; 128kJ
Storage In refrigerator for up to 3 months

glossary

allspice pimento.

beetroot also known as beets.

capsicum also known as bell pepper or, simply, pepper.

cardamom seeds native to India and used extensively in its cuisine; can be purchased in pod, seed or ground form. Has an aromatic, sweetly rich flavour and is one of the world's most expensive spices.

chilli available in many different types and sizes. Use rubber gloves when seeding and chopping fresh chillies as they can burn your skin. Removing seeds and membranes lessens the heat level.

banana: thick-fleshed sweet chilli, having a similar flavour to a capsicum.

powder: crushed dried chillies blended to a powder.

thai: small, medium-to-hot chilli that ranges from bright-red to dark-green in colour.

choko also known as chayote and christophene; a vegetable with pale-green spiky skin.

cornflour also known as cornstarch; used as a thickening agent in cooking.

cucumber

gherkin: miniature cucumber.

green: long, oval-shaped fat cucumber.

lebanese: long, slender and thin-skinned; also known as the European or burpless cucumber.

cumin seeds aromatic and nutty, cumin seeds are the dried fruit of a plant from the parsley family; also available in ground form.

dates fruit from the date palm; have brown paper-thin skin and sticky, sweet flesh with a long seed. Available fresh or dried (seeded or unseeded).

eggplant also known as aubergine.

baby: small, finger-shaped eggplant with dark-purple glossy skin.

five-spice a fragrant mixture of ground cinnamon, cloves, star anise, Sichuan pepper and fennel seeds.

flour, plain an all-purpose flour, made from wheat.

lemon grass a tall, clumping, lemon-smelling and -tasting, sharp-edged grass; the white lower part of each stem is chopped and used in Asian cooking or for tea.

mixed spice a blend of ground spices usually consisting of cinnamon, allspice and nutmeg.

mustard

dijon: a pale brown, distinctively flavoured, fairly mild French mustard.

powder: finely ground mustard seeds.

seeded: also known as wholegrain; a French-style coarse-grain mustard made from crushed mustard seeds and Dijon-style French mustard.

seeds, black and yellow: acrid seeds from any of several species of mustard plants; used for pickling, as a seasoning in savoury dishes, to make freshly ground mustard, and as an ingredient in salad dressings.

oil

olive: mono-unsaturated oil made from the pressing of tree-ripened olives.

peanut: made from ground peanuts, peanut oil has a high smoking point; the most commonly used oil in Asian cooking.

vegetable: any of a number of oils sourced from plants rather than animal fats.

onion, red also known as Spanish, red Spanish or Bermuda onion; a sweet-flavoured, large, purple-red onion that is particularly good eaten raw in salads.

pawpaw also known as papaya; thin-skinned tropical fruit, the ripe flesh of which varies from orange to yellow to pink in colour. Green pawpaw is a popular ingredient in curries and chutney.

quince large, yellow-skinned, fragrant fruit with crunchy cream flesh that, when slow-cooked, turns a deep ruby-red in colour.

rhubarb vegetable (though eaten as a fruit) with cherry-red stalks and green leaves. The stalks are the only edible part of rhubarb; the leaves contain oxalic acid and are toxic.

sugar we used coarse, granulated table sugar, also known as crystal sugar, unless otherwise specified.

brown: an extremely soft, finely granulated sugar retaining molasses for its characteristic colour and flavour.

caster: also known as superfine or finely granulated table sugar.

palm: very fine sugar from the coconut palm. It is sold in cakes, and is also known as gula jawa, gula melaka and jaggery. Palm sugar can be replaced with brown or black sugar.

raw: natural brown granulated sugar.

sultanas golden raisins.

tamarind

concentrate: thick paste made from the acid-tasting fruit of the tamarind tree. To dilute, follow instructions on packet.

dried: the reddish-brown pulp, stones, rind and roots of the bean of the tamarind tree. To extract its acidic, sour essence, soak in boiling water until cool then press though a sieve back into the soaking water; use the flavoured water and discard the pulp.

tomato

green: medium-sized tomato with piquant flavour; well suited to relishes.

paste: triple-concentrated tomato puree used to flavour soups, stews and sauces.

treacle thick, dark syrup not unlike molasses; a by-product from sugar refining.

vinegar

balsamic: authentic only from the province of Modena, Italy; made from wine of white Trebbiano grapes and aged in antique wooden casks.

cider: made from fermented apples.

malt: made from fermented malted barley and beech shavings.

red wine: based on fermented red wine.

white: made from spirit of cane sugar.

white wine: made from fermented white wine.

index

facts and figures 63

These conversions are approximate only, but the difference between an exact and the approximate conversion of various liquid and dry measures is minimal and will not affect your cooking results.

Measuring equipment

The difference between one country's measuring cups and another's is, at most, within a 2 or 3 teaspoon variance. (For the record, 1 Australian metric measuring cup holds approximately 250ml.) The most accurate way of measuring dry ingredients is to weigh them. For liquids, use a clear glass or plastic jug having metric markings.

Note: NZ, Canada, USA and UK all use 15ml tablespoons. Australian tablespoons measure 20ml.
All cup and spoon measurements are level.

How to measure

When using graduated measuring cups, shake dry ingredients loosely into the appropriate cup. Do not tap the cup on a bench or tightly pack the ingredients unless directed to do so. Level the top of measuring cups and measuring spoons with a knife. When measuring liquids, place a clear glass or plastic jug having metric markings on a flat surface to check accuracy at eye level.

Dry Measures

metric	imperial
15g	$1/2$oz
30g	1oz
60g	2oz
90g	3oz
125g	4oz ($1/4$lb)
155g	5oz
185g	6oz
220g	7oz
250g	8oz ($1/2$lb)
280g	9oz
315g	10oz
345q	11oz
375g	12oz ($3/4$lb)
410g	13oz
440g	14oz
470g	15oz
500g	16oz (1lb)
750g	24oz ($1^1/2$lb)
1kg	32oz (2lb)

We use large eggs having an average weight of 60g.

Liquid Measures

metric	imperial
30ml	1 fluid oz
60ml	2 fluid oz
100ml	3 fluid oz
125ml	4 fluid oz
150ml	5 fluid oz ($1/4$ pint/1 gill)
190ml	6 fluid oz
250ml (1cup)	8 fluid oz
300ml	10 fluid oz ($1/2$ pint)
500ml	16 fluid oz
600ml	20 fluid oz (1 pint)
1000ml (1litre)	$1^3/4$ pints

Helpful Measures

metric	imperial
3mm	$1/8$in
6mm	$1/4$in
1cm	$1/2$in
2cm	$3/4$in
2.5cm	1in
6cm	$2^1/2$in
8cm	3in
20cm	8in
23cm	9in
25cm	10in
30cm	12in (1ft)

Oven Temperatures

These oven temperatures are only a guide. Always check the manufacturer's manual.

	°C (Celsius)	°F (Fahrenheit)	Gas Mark
Very slow	120	250	1
Slow	150	300	2
Moderately slow	160	325	3
Moderate	180 –190	350 – 375	4
Moderately hot	200 – 210	400 – 425	5
Hot	220 – 230	450 – 475	6
Very hot	240 – 250	500 – 525	7

Food editor Pamela Clark
Associate food editor Karen Hammial
Assistant food editor Kathy McGarry
Assistant recipe editor Elizabeth Hooper

HOME LIBRARY STAFF
Editor-in-chief Mary Coleman
Managing editor (food) Susan Tomnay
Marketing manager Nicole Pizanis
Editor Julie Collard
Concept design Jackie Richards
Designer Mary Keep
Group publisher Jill Baker
Chief executive officer John Alexander

Produced by *The Australian Women's Weekly*
Home Library, Sydney.

Colour separations by
ACP Colour Graphics Pty Ltd, Sydney.
Printing by Dai Nippon Printing, Korea

Published by ACP Publishing Pty Limited,
54 Park St, Sydney; GPO Box 4088, Sydney,
NSW 1028. Ph: (02) 9282 8618
Fax: (02) 9267 9438.

AWWHomeLib@publishing.acp.com.au

Australia Distributed by Network Distribution
Company, GPO Box 4088, Sydney, NSW 1028.
Ph: (02) 9282 8777 Fax: (02) 9264 3278.

United Kingdom Distributed by Australian
Consolidated Press (UK), Moulton Park Business
Centre, Red House Road, Moulton Park,
Northampton, NN3 6AQ. Ph: (01604) 497 531
Fax: (01604) 497 533 Acpukltd@aol.com

Canada Distributed by Whitecap Books Ltd,
351 Lynn Ave, North Vancouver, BC, V7J 2C4,
Ph: (604) 980 9852.

New Zealand Distributed by Netlink Distribution
Company, Level 4, 23 Hargreaves St,
College Hill, Auckland 1, Ph: (9) 302 7616.

South Africa Distributed by:
PSD Promotions (Pty) Ltd, PO Box 1175,
Isando 1600, SA, Ph: (011) 392 6065; and
CNA Limited, Newsstand Division, PO Box 10799,
Johannesburg 2000, SA, Ph: (011) 491 7500.

Creative food: Pickles and Chutneys

Includes index.
ISBN 1 86396 206 9

1. Pickles. 2. Chutneys. 3. Cookery.
I. Title: Australian Women's Weekly.
(Series: Australian Women's Weekly
creative food mini series).
641.812

© ACP Publishing Pty Limited 2000
ACN 053 273 546
ABN 18 053 273 546

Cover: Mushrooms with bite, page 27.
Stylist Carolyn Fienberg
Photographer Scott Cameron
Back cover: Quince paste, page 7.

The publishers would like to thank The Art of
Wine and Food; The Bay Tree Kitchen Shop;
Empire Homewares; The Family Jewels; Kings,
Queens & Soup Tureens; and Mud Australia
for props used in photography.

mini books